Building Homes

Graham Rickard

Lerner Publications Company
Minneapolis

All words printed in **bold** are explained
in the glossary on page 30.

Cover illustration *Building apartments on a construction
site in West Germany*

First published in the U.S. in 1989 by Lerner Publications
Company. All U.S. rights reserved. No part of this book
may be reproduced or transmitted in any form or by any
means, electronic or mechanical, including photocopying
and recording, or by any information storage or retrieval
system, without permission in writing from the publisher
except for the inclusion of brief quotations in an
acknowledged review.
Copyright © 1988 Wayland (Publishers) Ltd., Hove, East
Sussex. First published 1988 by Wayland (Publishers) Ltd.

Library of Congress Cataloging-in-Publication Data

Rickard, Graham.
  Building homes/Graham Rickard.
  p.   cm.
  Bibliography: p.
  Includes index.
  Summary: Describes how people in different parts of the world
build their homes using local materials available to them.
  ISBN 0-8225-2129-6 (lib. bdg.)
  1. House construction—Juvenile literature. | 1. House
construction. 2. Dwellings. | I. Title
TH4811.5.R53   1989
690′.537—dc 19   88-21442
                                                      CIP
                                                       AC

Printed in Italy by G. Canale & C.S.p.A., Turin
Bound in the United States of America

1 2 3 4 5 6 7 8 9 10 98 97 96 95 94 93 92 91 90 89

Contents

What is home?

For survival and comfort, many animals need homes to protect them from the weather and their enemies. In spite of the technological advances that humans have made, we still have the same two basic needs as other creatures—food and shelter.

Our homes are places where we feel safe to eat, sleep, relax, raise children, and keep our belongings in comfort and in private.

The first human shelters were caves or simple huts of stones and branches. Over the centuries, our building skills progressed a great deal. New materials and building techniques make today's homes more efficient and comfortable than ever before.

Throughout the world, people live in many different types of homes. These vary according to the climate, the building materials available, whether the people are rich or poor, and what their needs and patterns of life are.

Wherever they live, people have always found ways of using local

Left Apartment buildings on the coast of Sydney, Australia

4

Right Some people live in unusual homes such as these floating houses in Vancouver, Canada.

Below Because of the high cost of land in cities, many city-dwellers around the world live in high-rises similar to these in West Berlin.

materials to build safe homes for themselves and their families. Local conditions influence the homes they build, so while some people live in high-rise apartments, others live underground or on the water in floating homes. All these homes may look very different, but they all fill the same basic human needs of shelter, safety, and comfort.

Building with wood

Wood is more plentiful and cheaper than other building materials. It is light, strong, and easy to cut and shape with simple tools. Wood can be joined with glue, nails, screws, ropes, metal fasteners, or joints.

Wood looks attractive, **insulates** well against heat and cold, and, if properly cared for, will last a very long time. Floors, walls, and roofs, as well as window frames, doors, and many other parts of a house can be made from wood. It is used in more ways than any other building material.

All lumber is divided into two types: hardwood, from broad-leaved trees, such as birch, maple, and oak; and softwood, from cone-bearing trees, such as hemlock and pine. The cheaper softwoods can easily be sawed, bored, chiseled, and planed, so they are often used for construction. Hardwoods are usually heavier and more durable, but they are more expensive. They are often used for furniture, cabinets, paneling, and floors.

One method of building with wood is to stack whole tree trunks on top of each other with notches in the ends to hold them together. When the United States was being settled and trees were plentiful,

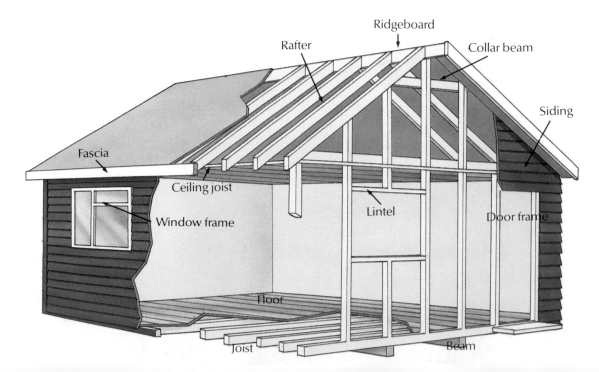

people built log cabins like this. Although this method is simpler than others, a lot of lumber is wasted.

Lumber can be saved by sawing tree trunks into planks for different uses. Larger planks are used to build the frame of a house, which is covered with **sheathing** and then **siding**. Siding may be brick, stone, aluminum, or wood. Sheathing may be wood paneling, plywood, or fiberboard. In the United States today, the sheathing most commonly used is plasterboard, which is called by its trademark, Sheetrock. To make plywood and fiberboard, strips or chips of wood can be pressed into shape with glue.

Above At this building site in California, the basic material used for building is wood.

Left This diagram shows the parts of a house that can be built with wood.

Right This wood house is typical of homes in the southern United States.

7

Using plant and animal materials

Trees provide not only lumber, but also branches, twigs, leaves, and bark, all of which can be used for building houses. In Thailand and parts of Africa, walls are made by weaving twigs around upright poles set in the ground. To make the walls weatherproof, they are covered with a mixture of mud and clay. The whole framework is called **wattle and daub**.

Grass, sod, moss, heather, and reeds are all used for building materials, especially watertight roofs, wherever they grow in large quantities. Overlapping bundles of reeds or straw, held in place with split twigs, are used to make thatched roofs.

In Ireland and Scandinavia, special spades are used to cut long strips of sod. Pieces of sod can be laid on top of one another like bricks to build walls or spread across a wooden frame to make a roof that is warm and waterproof.

On the desert of northern Africa, people weave mats of grass to cover a framework of wooden poles. These light shelters protect them from the blazing sun.

In the marshlands of southern Iraq live the Ma'dan people. They cut large reeds, up to 23 feet (7 m) long,

Wood frame

Wattle

Daub

Left Mud is plastered over a framework of woven sticks to make this wattle and daub home in Kenya.

Right Long strips of woven cloth are sewn together to make Bedouin tents.

Left This diagram shows the structure of wattle and daub.

Below The Ma'dan build homes using giant reeds.

and tie them together in bundles. They set the ends of each bundle into holes in the ground to make the tunnel shape of a house. The floor, walls, and roof are made of mats woven from reeds.

The hair from sheep, goats, and camels can be woven into fabric to make tents. The nomadic Bedouin tribes on African and Middle Eastern deserts live in such tents.

The nomads of Mongolia and Iran live in circular yurts, which are tents built by covering a lattice frame with felt made from pressed animal hairs.

9

Building with mud and clay

Above This woman is mixing clay with water and smoothing the surface with a trowel to repair the wall of an adobe house in New Mexico. The walls dry hard in the sun.

In countries throughout the world, clay and mud have always been used to build walls and floors. Mud is most suited to hot, dry climates, rather than cool or wet climates, since it is quickly washed away by heavy rain.

African mud houses are made from soil mixed with water. The mud is then shaped by hand until the circular walls reach the right height. Small doors and windows are cut when the mud is still damp, and the thatched roof is added when the walls have hardened in the sun.

Arab builders use mud bricks to build thick-walled houses with only tiny windows. The windows let in some light but keep out the heat of the sun's rays.

In Mexico and the southwestern United States, clay blocks are dried in the sun to make **adobe** walls. Slip, or liquid clay, holds the blocks together and gives the walls a smooth finish.

Mud or clay can be made stronger by mixing it with materials such as straw, animal hair, or cow dung. In parts of Europe, such as southwest England, a mixture of clay, pebbles, sand, and straw, called cob, is used to make walls. Each layer is left to dry before the next is added. A sharp spade is used to cut the doors and windows, and the walls are given a waterproof coating of tar or lime.

In developing countries, where concrete and bricks are often too expensive, a new tool may provide an answer to people's housing needs. A simple hand press has been invented which uses a mixture of soil and cement or lime to produce strong, regular soil blocks. These can be used in the same way as bricks. The new blocks last up to 30 years, and have already been used to build new villages in Kenya, Nigeria, and the Caribbean.

Below This country cottage in southwest England has cob walls. Cob is a mixture of materials such as clay, straw, and sand that is covered with a waterproof coating.

Above This blockmaking machine is operated by hand to make building blocks from soil.

Building with stone

Stone is the most durable of all building materials. Wherever there is a local supply, it has always been used to build solid, long-lasting houses. But stone is expensive because it is difficult to quarry, or remove from the ground, and it is also difficult to cut.

There are two types of building stone: ashlar and rubble. Ashlar is stone that is cut and shaped into regular blocks. It can be used to build a whole house or just to strengthen corners and areas surrounding the door and windows. Rubble buildings are made of rough, natural lumps of stone which may be laid in layers, or **courses**, or piled up to make a wall.

Stonework and brickwork is called masonry. A stonemason usually uses a **mortar** made from sand and lime or cement to stick the stones together.

Limestone and sandstone are good for building with because they are easily cut and shaped with a mason's hammer and chisel, but hard enough to stand up to rain and frost.

Granite is a very hard stone that can only be used in large square blocks. But because it is so strong, it has been used in the construction of many public buildings.

Left In this small quarry in Kenya, the quarriers are using a variety of hand tools to remove lumps of stone from the ground. One quarrier is squaring off the stones and giving them a smooth finish.

Both slate and flint are fine-grained. They can be split into thin pieces, which are often used for roofing and flooring tiles.

Marble is the most elegant of building stones. It can be finely carved into delicate shapes that decorate stairways, walls, floors, and fireplaces.

Slabs of natural stone make an attractive finish for modern high-rise buildings. Recently, builders have used crushed stone mixed with cement to produce molded building blocks. This is cheaper and easier to use than natural stone.

Above This French slate quarrier taps the slate with a heavy tool and the stone splits cleanly into thin sheets.

Left Knapped flint, split to show a dark, shiny surface, covers the lower half of the wall.

Building with bricks

Bricks are rectangular blocks of clay, which are left to dry and then fired in a very hot oven, or kiln. Bricks were the first manufactured building materials, molded by hand thousands of years ago. Later, rectangular wooden molds were used to make bricks more regular in size and shape. Hand-molded bricks are still made in many countries including India and Malawi.

Modern brick **extrusion** machines squeeze out clay in long strips. The strips are sliced to the right size with wires. Standard building bricks measure 2¼ x 3¾ x 8 inches (5.7 x 9.5 x 20 cm)—a size which comfortably fits the adult human hand.

It is easier to build with bricks than with stone, but the techniques are similar. A bricklayer lays the bricks in courses and sticks them together with mortar, which forms joints between them. The vertical joints overlap to strengthen the wall.

Brick walls can be built only a few courses at a time so that the wall does not lose its shape under the weight of the bricks while the mortar is still soft. The bricklayer often uses a **level** and **plumb line** to make sure that the courses are even and the wall is vertical.

Bricks laid with their long sides exposed are called stretchers, and bricks laid with their short ends

Right This Mexican builder is using a rectangular hand mold to make regular-shaped bricks.

exposed are called headers. Low-quality bricks, or common bricks, are used for inner walls, and the highest-quality and most attractive bricks, or face bricks, are used for outer walls. Some bricks have holes in them, which makes them lighter and saves clay.

Engineering bricks are strong enough to be used in the **foundations** and **footings** that support an entire building. Refractory bricks are fired under extremely high temperatures to make them more durable. They are used in building fireplaces and industrial furnaces. Thin refractories are even used to cover the outside of the space shuttles to protect the shuttles from extreme heat and cold.

Above *Freshly-made bricks are being stacked onto a wheelbarrow at a brick factory in Brazil.*

Right *A builder uses a stretched piece of string to make sure that a course is perfectly even.*

Building with concrete

Concrete is a mixture of cement, sand, gravel, and water. The cement acts as a glue that sticks the stones in the gravel together, and the sand fills in any spaces between the stones. Concrete dries rock hard, but while it is still wet it can be sprayed into shape or poured into molds.

Because it is so strong, fairly small concrete sections can be used to support very large weights. Concrete is an ideal material for building skyscrapers and blocks of apartments and office buildings.

Reinforced, or strengthened, concrete is even stronger. It is made by pouring concrete around steel mesh or bars. When the steel bars are stretched until the concrete sets, pre-stressed concrete is made. Other materials, such as glass fiber or plastic, are also used to make the concrete stronger.

On a building site, small amounts of concrete are mixed by hand, but larger amounts are delivered ready-mixed and then poured or pumped from a truck. Wood or metal **forms** are used to shape the concrete on site. When the concrete has set, the forms are removed and used for the next section of the building.

Sometimes the concrete sections are delivered ready-made from the factory. This saves the construction workers time on the building site. Concrete can also be made into blocks, which are much larger and much quicker to build with than bricks.

Lightweight blocks, which are often used to build the inner walls of a house, are made by using lightweight shales, ash, and pumice instead of the heavier gravel and sand. Or chemicals may be used that foam to produce air bubbles in the concrete as it hardens. Concrete blocks are good for insulating houses against heat loss and outside noise.

Above *Ready-mixed concrete is poured from a truck into wooden forms.*

Left *A cement factory in Sicily*

Right *The strength of concrete makes it an ideal material for building skyscrapers.*

Building with metal

In most houses, there are metal nails and screws, hinges, window frames, wires, and pipes, but it is only recently that metal has been used to give a house its structure.

Reinforced steel **joists** are built into some houses to support the weight over a door or window opening. But steel **girder construction** is usually only seen in modern high-rise buildings. For its weight, steel is a very strong material. A steel framework acts as a skeleton that supports the weight of the whole building. The walls do not have to support anything. They just cover the steel framework.

For added strength, the sections of girders, or I beams, are made in an H shape. They are bolted, **riveted**, or welded together to form the vertical and horizontal supports for each floor, which is usually made from concrete. The outer walls, which act as a skin to protect the building, can be made of brick, glass, stone, sheet metal, or any other material.

Using a crane to lift the heavy girders into position, the construction crew builds each story up in a series of box shapes. Sometimes the

central crane tower is left in the building to form the elevator shaft for a large high rise.

Throughout the world, poor people live just outside large cities in **shanty** towns. They build their homes with whatever building materials they can find.

They often use corrugated metal sheets as a cheap form of roofing. If a family is forced to move to another area, they may take their roof with them.

Left *A welder uses the heat from a gas torch to cut through a steel girder.*

Right *A steel girder framework acts as a skeleton to support the weight of a high-rise building.*

Below *This shanty town with corrugated iron roofs is in a city suburb in Brazil.*

Preparing the site

In many parts of the world, family and friends still help people to build their their own homes. They use traditional designs and are skilled at using local materials. However, building a house using modern methods requires the skills of many different people.

First, the building site must be measured and surveyed. The surveyor uses tape measures, **theodolites**, and levels to produce a site plan that shows the size and shape of the plot.

The **architect** works from the site plan to design the house, making detailed drawings of every part of the building. These plans are checked by the local housing authority, which then gives permission for work to proceed.

Large earth-moving machines clear and level the site. The site supervisor watches as the foundations of the walls are marked out with strings and wooden pegs according to measurements made with surveying instruments. Mechanical excavators, or digging machines, dig trenches for the foundations of the house. If there is a basement, the foundations are beneath it. The foundations must be strong enough to keep the house from sinking into the ground. They must also reach below the frost line so the house will not rise and fall when the ground freezes and thaws.

Right The supervisor is surveying the site with a level to measure the height of the land at different points.

Concrete is poured into the trenches and sets to form a solid foundation. The ground floor or the basement is dug out and partially filled with a **hard core** of brick and stone rubble. This is covered with a layer of concrete or laid with joists to support a wooden floor.

On top of the foundations, bricklayers use strong engineering bricks to lay the underground footings for the outer walls. If there is a basement, concrete is poured into molds to form the basement walls.

Above Liquid concrete is poured into the trenches to form a solid foundation.

Right Concrete joists are laid to support the ground floor.

Building the walls

In many developed countries, houses are built of bricks. The bricklayer lays the corners of each wall and then stretches a string line between them as a guide for laying each course of bricks.

Outside walls are sometimes built with a gap, or cavity, in the middle. The outer "skin" must be much thicker than the walls dividing the rooms. Face bricks should be used for the outer skin, while the inner wall can be made of common bricks or concrete blocks. For added strength, the two walls are joined with metal ties and the cavity is sometimes filled with insulation material.

After the first few courses of bricks, bricklayers in some countries, such as Great Britain, put down a layer of slate or tarred felt, called a damp-proof course. The damp-proof course stops the wall from soaking up the moisture in the ground. For

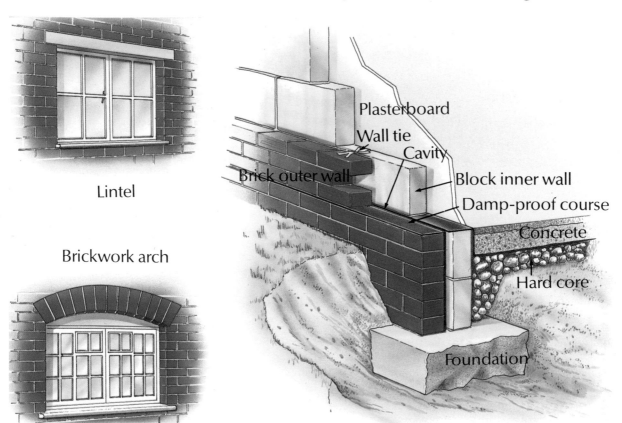

Lintel

Brickwork arch

Plasterboard

Wall tie

Cavity

Brick outer wall

Block inner wall

Damp-proof course

Concrete

Hard core

Foundation

the same reason, polyethylene, a type of waterproof plastic, is laid under concrete floors.

Carpenters put the door and window frames in the gaps left by the bricklayers. Brick arches or concrete **lintels** are laid above each door or window opening to support the weight of the wall above.

Before the mortar sets too hard between the bricks, it is rubbed and pointed with a small trowel to give it a smooth, waterproof joint.

Frame houses need only a thin outer skin of brick to protect the wood. The inside is covered with a layer of plasterboard.

Wood frames are usually delivered in ready-made sections. In some modern factories, tree trunks are fed in at one end and complete houses come out at the other!

Above In south Tanzania, a builder uses mud to hold the large homemade bricks together to build a wall.

Left A bricklayer builds a cavity wall with insulation on a steel-framed building.

Building the roof

The roof is the most difficult part of most houses to build. Flat roofs are suitable in dry climates, where they often provide extra living or storage space. In areas where there is more rain, however, roofs are usually slanted to allow water to run off easily into the gutters. Most roofs are built with overhanging **eaves** to protect the walls, and slanting roofs have gables, which are the triangular walls at either end of the roof. A roof is usually made of a wood framework covered with waterproof materials.

On top of the brick walls, a carpenter lays a piece of wood called a wall plate. The ceiling joists, which

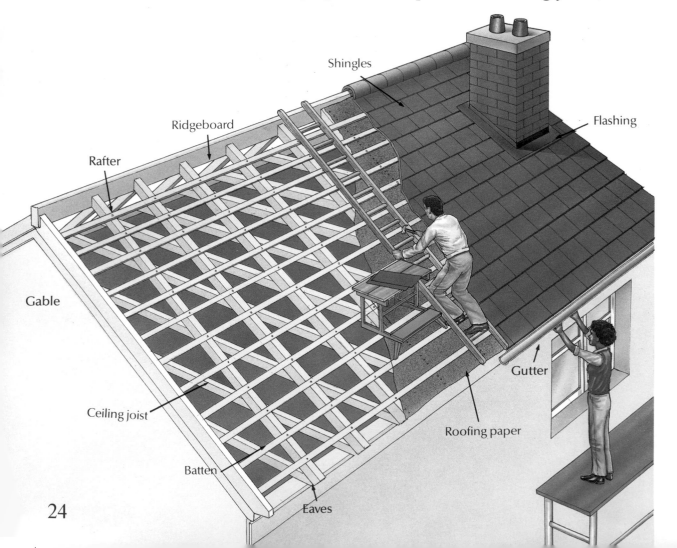

Shingles

Ridgeboard

Flashing

Rafter

Gable

Ceiling joist

Batten

Eaves

Gutter

Roofing paper

Right To make a thatched roof, the thatcher fastens overlapping bundles of straw to the battens.

Left One builder attaches shingles to wooden battens while another puts the gutters in place underneath the eaves.

go on top of the wall plate, will support the ceiling of the rooms below and the attic floor.

The wooden beams that make the sloping **rafters** are cut to the right shape and length and nailed into place. Each pair of rafters is joined at the top to the **ridgeboard** and at the bottom to the wall plate. A horizontal **brace** connects each pair of rafters to make an A shape. This gives the roof added strength.

The framework is then covered with overlapping layers of roofing paper. Wooden **battens** are nailed across the length of the roof to support the final layer of siding, which can be wooden shingles, clay tiles, slates, or thatch.

Strips of lead **flashing** are used to waterproof joints wherever the roof meets a chimney.

Gutters and downspouts, made of aluminum or plastic, are put in place around the bottom of the roof to drain away rain and melted snow.

Light, heat, and water

People need shelter. They also need heat to cook food and to keep them warm, water for drinking and washing, and light for the hours of darkness.

In modern houses throughout the world, heat, water, and light are available by turning on a faucet or flicking a switch. Electricity and water and gas lines, together with flush toilets and good sewage systems to carry away human waste, have improved standards of comfort and cleanliness over the last century.

Behind the walls and under the floorboards, plumbers put in a

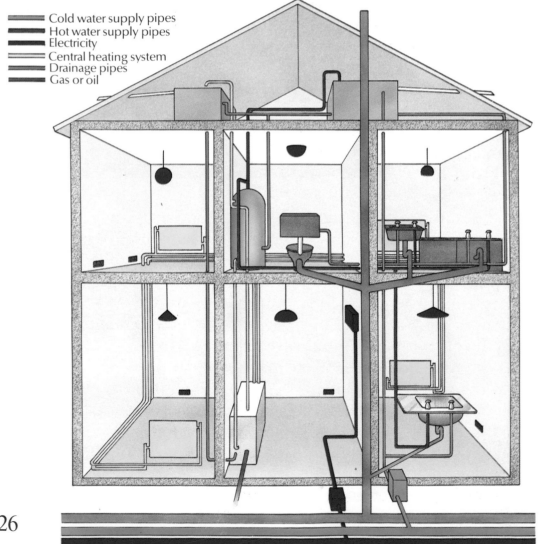

Cold water supply pipes
Hot water supply pipes
Electricity
Central heating system
Drainage pipes
Gas or oil

complicated system of copper or plastic pipes to carry water through the house. Water enters underground through the water supply pipe and is carried up to a large water tank. From the tank, the water is fed to all the faucets, toilets, and hot water tanks. A smaller tank feeds the boiler and radiators of the central heating system. There is a main valve on the water supply pipe to turn off the entire water supply to the house.

Waste water from sinks, baths, and toilets flows through a separate system of larger pipes and is carried underground to the main sewage system.

The electrician lays two sets of cables around the house. One set is for lighting. The other carries a larger current, or flow of electricity, to power sockets for refrigerators, televisions, and other appliances. All the circuits are connected to the main electricity supply, which enters the house through a meter and circuit breaker or a fuse box.

If the house is heated by hot water, the hot water is fed around the house in pipes. If it is heated by air, warm air from the furnace is blown through pipes into each room.

Left *This simplified diagram shows the plumbing and electricity in a house.*

Right *This house in the United States is heated by solar power from solar panels on the roof.*

27

The finishing touches

When the walls and roof have been built, there is still a lot of work to do before the house is finished.

Carpenters fit doors and windows into their frames and build the wooden stairs. Wooden or plaster molding is installed to cover the joint where a wall meets the ceiling, and baseboards are nailed around the bottom of the walls.

Above *An electrician wires a socket to the cables in the wall.*

Left *A glazier puts a pane of glass in a window frame. The putty around the frame will harden and hold the glass in place.*

Left To prevent water or grease from damaging the walls, a decorator places ceramic tiles around the sink. When the tiles are dry, a thin layer of cement will be pushed between the tiles to keep the water out.

The seams between the pieces of plasterboard are taped and then smoothed over so the walls and ceiling have an even finish. Glaziers use putty to fit the glass into the window frames.

Plumbers connect the bathtubs, showers, and sinks to the water pipes. Electricians wire light fixtures and switches to the cables in the wall. The central heating system is tested and telephone and television cables are installed.

After this, the decorators can begin. In bathrooms and kitchens, they cover the walls around showers and sinks with ceramic tiles to prevent water damage.

Decorators use different types of paint for different areas. Latex paint is ideal for inner walls and ceilings. It can be applied with a brush or a roller. Ceilings are often given a rough finish by using a thicker paint. Gloss paint is shiny and waterproof —excellent for use on outside woodwork, as well as doors and windows inside the house. Exterior wall paint gives a tough finish which will last for many years.

Once the floor has been laid and carpets, tiles, wood, or vinyl flooring put down, the house can finally be called a home. The new owners can move in.

Glossary

adobe Brick that has been dried and hardened by the sun

architect A person who designs buildings

batten A long narrow piece of wood used to support material on a roof

brace Strengthening piece of iron or wood that connects pairs of rafters

course A row of bricks or stones in a wall

eaves The part of the roof that hangs over the outside wall

extrusion Shaping a material by forcing it under pressure through a hole—like toothpaste from a tube

flashing Strip of metal or lead used to prevent flooding or leaking from a joint

footings The wide base of a wall, built under ground level, on the foundations

forms Wood or metal molds for shaping liquid concrete

foundation The base on which the walls of a house stand, usually made by filling deep trenches with concrete

frost line The depth to which the ground freezes

girder construction Building with large steel beams

hard core Stones or rubble used as a foundation for buildings

insulation A material is used to stop heat or sound passing through the walls, doors, or windows of a house

joist Horizontal wooden or metal beam for supporting floors and roofs

level A straight bar of wood or metal with an air bubble trapped in liquid to show if a wall is level

lintel Horizontal beam above doors and windows to support a wall

mortar A mixture of sand, lime, and water used to hold bricks or stones together

plumbline A lead weight on a string, used to check whether a wall is exactly upright or whether it leans

rafters Sloping wood supports for the roof

ridgeboard Beam of wood along the top of the roof where the rafters meet

riveted Fastened together by a bolt called a rivet

shanty A makeshift house, often built from waste materials

sheathing The inner layer of the outside walls

siding The coating or covering put on the outside of a structure

theodolite A surveying instrument used to measure exact angles

wattle and daub Mud or clay, called daub, plastered onto a framework of woven sticks, or wattle

30

Books to read

Huts, Hovels & Houses by Timothy Fisher (Addison-Wesley, 1977)
Houses and Homes Around the World by Josphine Karavasil (Dillon Press, 1986)
The Rock Quarry Book by Michael Kehoe (Carolrhoda Books, 1981)
City: A Story of Roman Planning and Construction by David Macauley (Houghton Mifflin, 1974)
Unbuilding by David Macauley (Houghton Mifflin, 1980)
Grand Constructions by Gian Paolo Ceserani & Piero Ventura (G.P. Putnam's Sons, 1983)
Building a House by Ken Robbins (Four Winds, 1984)

Houses and Homes

Building Homes	Homes in Space
Castles and Mansions	Homes in the Future
Homes in Cold Places	Homes on Water
Homes in Hot Places	Mobile Homes

Picture acknowledgements

The author and publishers would like to thank the following for the illustrations in this book: Bryan and Cherry Alexander, p. 10; Building Research Station (Department of the Environment), p.11 (left); Cement and Concrete Association, p. 21; Bruce Coleman, p. 7 (top); Chris Fairclough, pp. 28, 30; Andy Hasson, p. 11 (right); The Hutchison Library, pp. 15 (top), 23 (top); Christine Osborne, pp. 8, 9 (bottom); Graham Rickard, pp. 13 (bottom), 20, 23 (bottom); Sefton, p. 17 (bottom); Topham, pp. 5 (bottom), 7 (bottom), 13 (top); ZEFA, pp. 4, 5 (top), 12, 14, 15 (bottom), 16, 17 (top), 18 (top), 19 (top), 25, 27; Laura Zito, p. 9 (top). All other pictures from the Wayland Picture Library. ZEFA, cover.

Index